Dino Duel

Velociraptor vs. Protoceratops

Prehistoric Showdown

Tom Jackson

Lerner Publications ◆ Minneapolis

Lerner Publications Company
An imprint of Lerner Publishing Group, Inc.
241 First Avenue North
Minneapolis, MN 55401 USA

For reading levels and more information, look up this title at www.lernerbooks.com.

Main body text set in Aptifer Sans LT Pro.
Typeface provided by Linotype.

Library of Congress Cataloging-in-Publication Data

Names: Jackson, Tom, 1972–author
Title: Velociraptor vs. protoceratops : prehistoric showdown / Tom Jackson.
Other titles: Velociraptor versus protoceratops
Description: Minneapolis : Lerner Publications, [2026] | Series: Dino duel | Includes bibliographical references and index. | Audience term: juvenile | Audience: Ages 8–11 Lerner Publications | Audience: Grades 4–6 Lerner Publications | Summary: "The velociraptor is small compared to the protoceratops, but in the fight to survive, the velociraptor might attack. Readers learn about these dinosaurs, and who might win in a fight"—Provided by publisher.
Identifiers: LCCN 2024049797 (print) | LCCN 2024049798 (ebook) | ISBN 9798765669273 (lib. bdg.) | ISBN 9798765683941 (pbk.) | ISBN 9798765676813 (epub)
Subjects: LCSH: Velociraptor—Juvenile literature | Protoceratops—Juvenile literature
Classification: LCC QE862.S3 J333 2026 (print) | LCC QE862.S3 (ebook) | DDC 567.912—dc23/eng/20250215

LC record available at https://lccn.loc.gov/2024049797
LC ebook record available at https://lccn.loc.gov/2024049798

Manufactured in the United States of America
1 – CG – 7/15/25

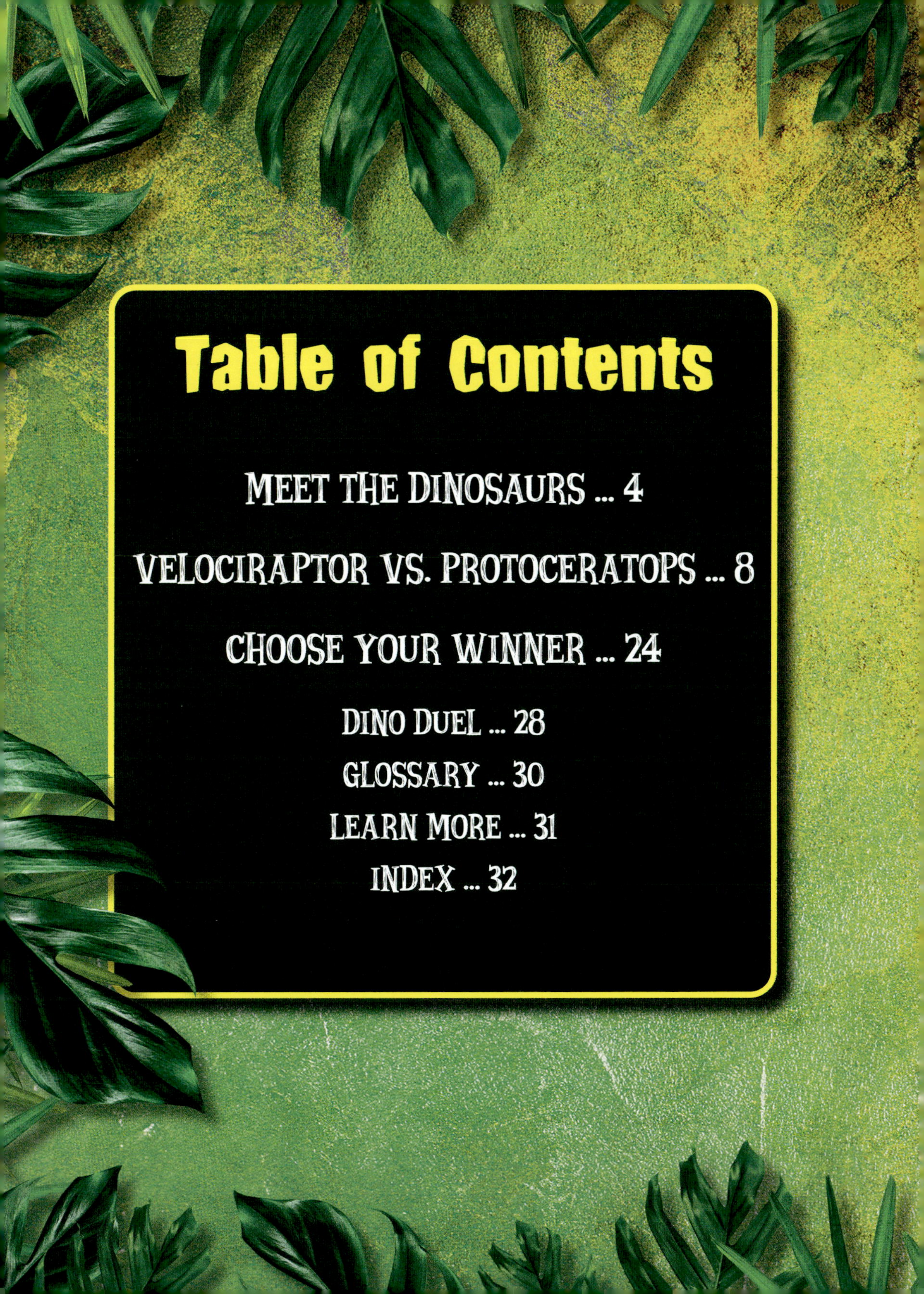

Table of Contents

MEET THE DINOSAURS

A velociraptor is on the hunt.

A velociraptor has been walking through a dry woodland for days. It is very hungry now. It has been searching everywhere for a small animal to eat. It looked in every bush and around the tufts of grass. It could not hear or smell any prey. The wind is picking up. Big clouds of dirt and dust are filling the sky.

Nearby, a group of mother protoceratops are guarding their nests. Their eggs are inside large mounds of earth. A few of the babies have hatched. They have broken out of their eggs and dug out of the dirt. These tiny baby protoceratops are too little to feed themselves or fight off a predator.

A protoceratops is ready to defend its nest from a velociraptor.

The velociraptor arrives at the protoceratops' nesting site. More babies are hatching out. Here is some food to eat at last! The velociraptor runs to grab a meal. But then an adult protoceratops stands in its way. There is going to be a fight!

The velociraptor has many teeth and thick, curved claws. The protoceratops is much bigger and has armored skin and a sharp, biting beak. Which one of these dinosaurs will win?

DINO STATS

Velociraptor

Weight: 15.5 pounds (7 kg)
Length: 6 feet (183 cm)
Main weapons: Hooked claws, sharp teeth, speed

Protoceratops

Weight: 53 pounds (24 kg)
Length: 4.5 feet (137 cm)
Main weapons: Neck frill made of bone, sharp beak

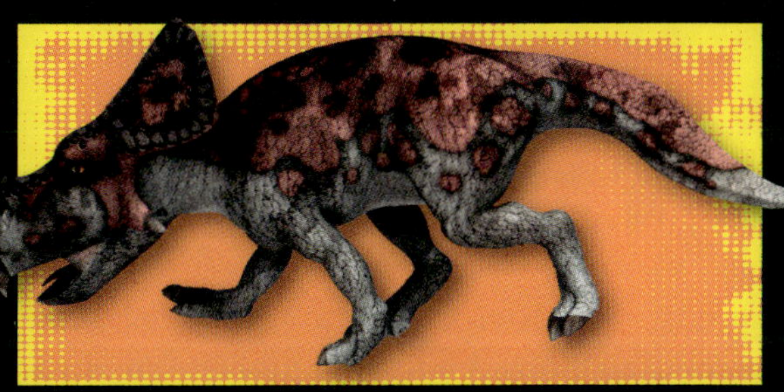

VELOCIRAPTOR VS PROTOCERATOPS

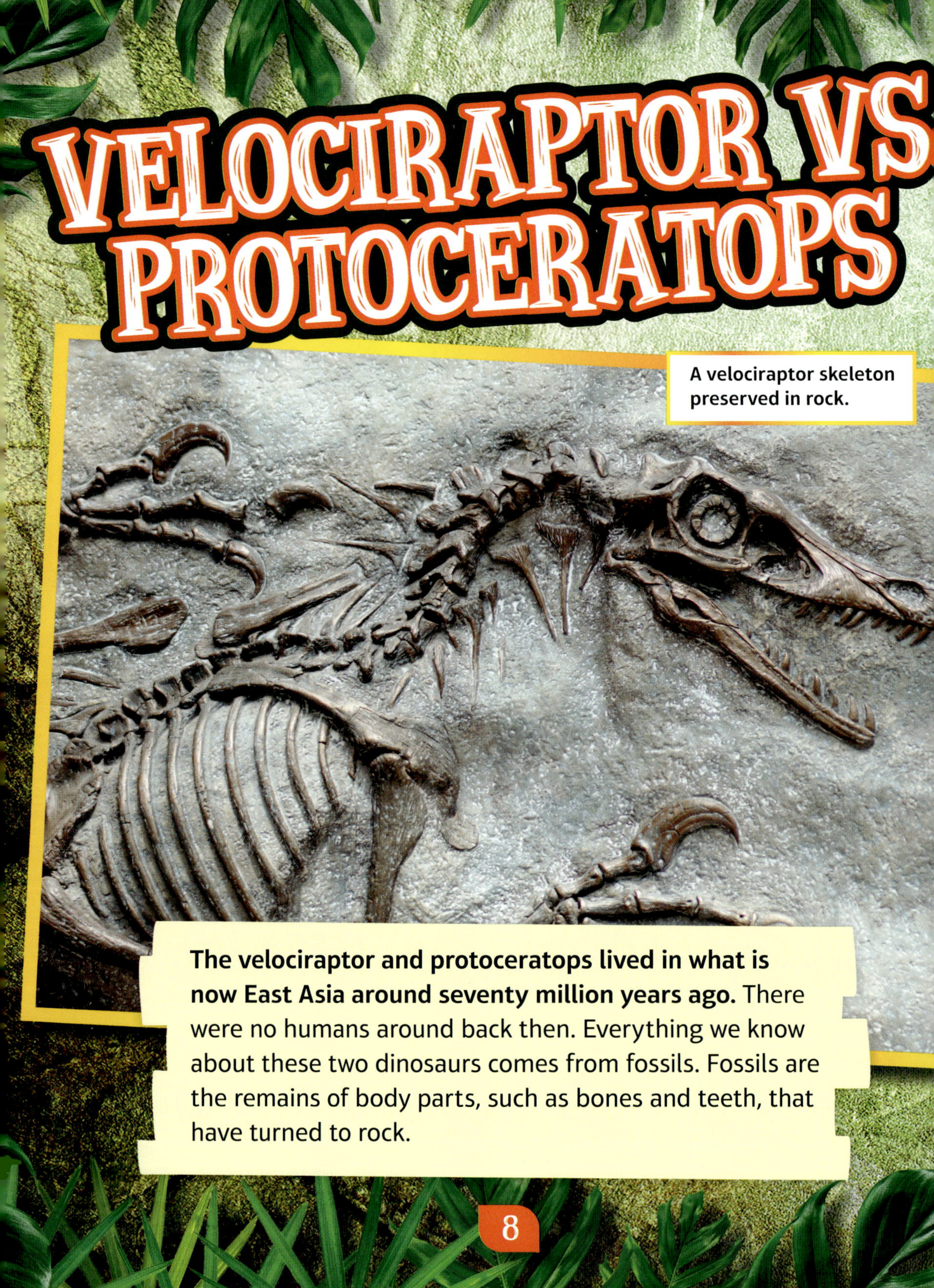

A velociraptor skeleton preserved in rock.

The velociraptor and protoceratops lived in what is now East Asia around seventy million years ago. There were no humans around back then. Everything we know about these two dinosaurs comes from fossils. Fossils are the remains of body parts, such as bones and teeth, that have turned to rock.

Scientists study the shape and size of the fossils to figure out how the dinosaurs lived when they were alive. The velociraptor was a small but fast-moving hunter. It ate small animals like lizards. The protoceratops was a plant-eater. It ate grass plants and the leaves from bushes.

A protoceratops skeleton on display in a museum

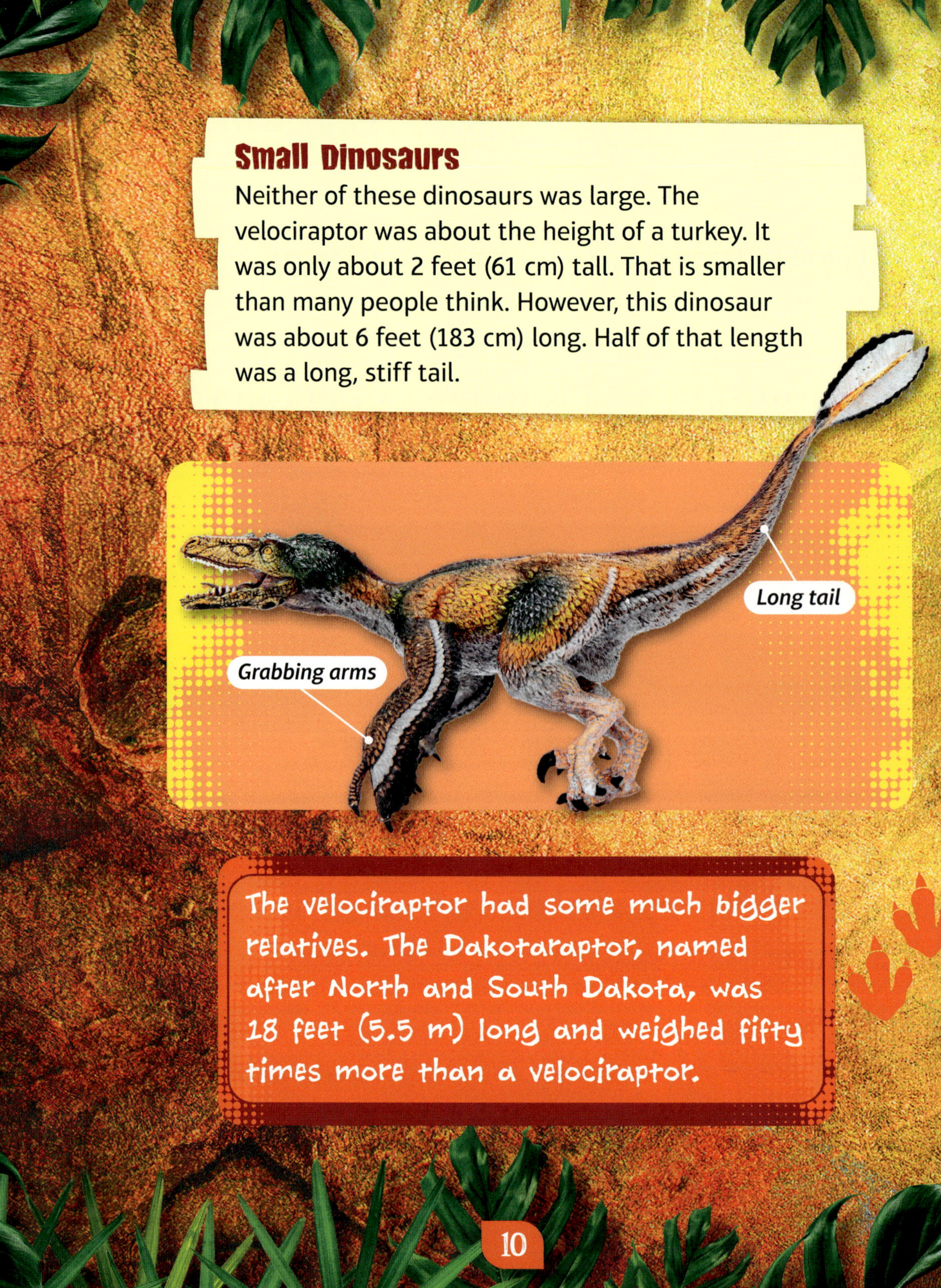

Small Dinosaurs

Neither of these dinosaurs was large. The velociraptor was about the height of a turkey. It was only about 2 feet (61 cm) tall. That is smaller than many people think. However, this dinosaur was about 6 feet (183 cm) long. Half of that length was a long, stiff tail.

The velociraptor had some much bigger relatives. The Dakotaraptor, named after North and South Dakota, was 18 feet (5.5 m) long and weighed fifty times more than a velociraptor.

A protoceratops was not quite as long as a velociraptor. Even so, this plant-eating dinosaur was much heavier and weighed as much as three velociraptors. An adult protoceratops was around the same size and weight as a Labrador retriever.

A velociraptor chased its prey, such as this small prehistoric mammal.

Running and Walking Speed

The velociraptor aways walked and ran on two legs. It could reach a top speed of 25 miles (40 km) an hour for short bursts. That was enough to outrun most other animals. The long tail kept the velociraptor balanced as it dashed forward. It also helped it steer at high speeds.

A protoceratops was much slower than a velociraptor. It walked at just 1.6 miles (2.6 km) per hour. That is half as fast as an adult can walk. The dinosaur could run at 10 miles (16 km) per hour for a short time. Scientists think that young protoceratops could stand up on their back legs when running fast. This was less easy for the adults.

A protoceratops standing on its back legs

The bones in a protoceratops's tail were quite tall. Scientists think this means the dinosaur stored fat in its tail for when there was no food around during a drought. This is similar to how a camel uses its hump today.

Hands and Feet

The velociraptor had twelve thick claws. There were three on each hand and foot. The claws on the hands were long and pointed. The foot claws were more hooked. The biggest claw was on the middle toe. This dinosaur could swipe down to slash at prey. It also used this claw to hold it down while ripping off chunks of meat with its teeth.

The name velociraptor means "quick thief." Scientists gave it this name because of how the dinosaur's arms were built for grabbing prey.

The protoceratops had strong legs for holding its heavy weight. The feet of a protoceratops had short toes that spread out to make the foot wider. Wide feet made it easier for the dinosaur to walk over soft soil and sand without sinking into it.

Mouth and Teeth

These two dinosaurs had very different ways of biting and eating food. The velociraptor was a meat-eater. It had around thirty small, hooked teeth. The hook shape helped the predator bite and grip its prey. Each of the velociraptor's teeth had sharp, saw-like edges that sliced into its food.

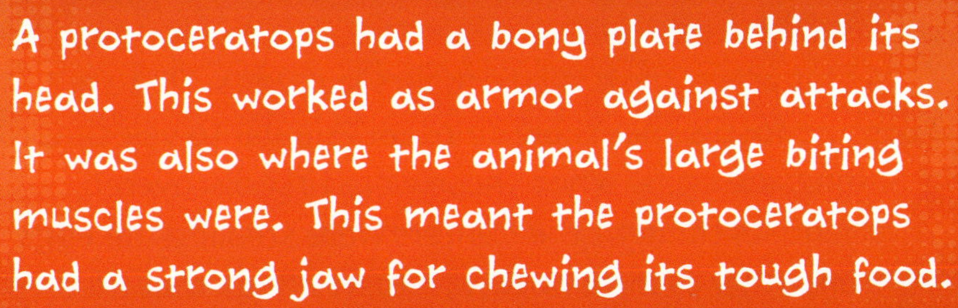

A protoceratops had a bony plate behind its head. This worked as armor against attacks. It was also where the animal's large biting muscles were. This meant the protoceratops had a strong jaw for chewing its tough food.

Beak

A protoceratops did not have any front teeth. Instead it had a beak made from sharp bone. The beak worked like scissor blades. It sliced through leaves and twigs. The protoceratops then used rows of very small teeth to grind up the food.

Laying Eggs

As far as we know, all dinosaurs laid eggs. There are some fossils that show dinosaurs similar to velociraptors alongside eggs. When these were first discovered, scientists thought the hunters were stealing the eggs from other dinosaurs. Now, experts think that these fossils show a nest. Velociraptors probably sat on their nests to keep their eggs warm like birds do today.

A velociraptor likely laid multiple eggs at once.

Protoceratops made round nests by making a pile of damp soil and sand. They laid their eggs on top and then covered them in more dirt. Other plant-eating dinosaurs that lived around this time gathered together in groups when making nests. They did this to protect their eggs from attack. It is possible that the protoceratops did this as well.

Baby protoceratops hatch from their long eggs.

A protoceratops's eggs were longer and narrower than a bird's egg. It took around eighty days for a baby to hatch out.

Stay Hidden

Small dinosaurs like the velociraptor and protoceratops needed ways to stay out of sight. The protoceratops was hiding from larger hunters such as the tarbosaurus, which was a relative of the T. rex. Scientists have suggested that protoceratops used their long back legs to dig burrows and pits. As well as being good hiding places, these homes would keep them cool on hot days.

The protoceratops lived in open places like dusty deserts.

Velociraptors could not fly, but other feathered dinosaurs could. These dinosaurs are related to today's birds.

Most velociraptor feathers were short and fluffy.

Velociraptors had feathers covering much of their body. They were probably there to keep the dinosaur warm. The longest feathers were on the arms. These arm feathers might have been brightly colored and used for making displays to other velociraptors. Or the dinosaur wrapped the feathers around their body. This helped them camouflage themselves and stay hidden.

Velociraptors would prey on injured animals that could not fight back.

Main Weapons

As a predator, the velociraptor had many ways of fighting other dinosaurs. It was a fast runner and very agile. It could jump high into the air. It would also grab prey with its hands and pin it to the ground with one of its hooked toe claws. The hunter then probably killed its prey by biting it.

Scientists used to think that a velociraptor's long toe claw was also used to slice into larger animals, like a protoceratops, and kill them. Scientists now think that the velociraptor could not do this.

A protoceratops was built to defend itself from bigger predators. These attackers would aim to bite the protoceratops's neck. This is one reason why the protoceratops had an armored frill of bone that covered this area. The frill was also used to show off to other protoceratops. The protoceratops with the biggest frills normally won in fights.

The protoceratops's frill gave it protection against attack.

CHOOSE YOUR WINNER

The hungry velociraptor wants to eat some baby protoceratops. However, their mother, a full-grown protoceratops, has come to fight back and save the babies. The velociraptor stops its attack. It turns around and runs back into the woodland. It flaps its feathered arms. They help to push it up the slope faster. It is too hungry to give up, so it will try something else.

The velociraptor runs back down toward the nests. It then jumps over the charging protoceratops. Its long tail helps it move in a straight line in the air. It lands safely on the other side of the protoceratops.

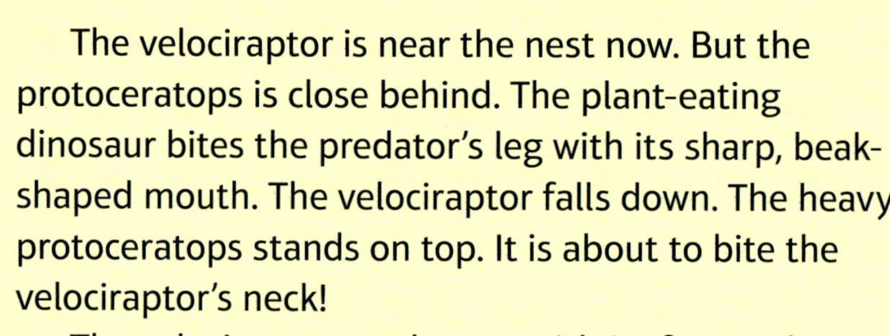

The velociraptor is near the nest now. But the protoceratops is close behind. The plant-eating dinosaur bites the predator's leg with its sharp, beak-shaped mouth. The velociraptor falls down. The heavy protoceratops stands on top. It is about to bite the velociraptor's neck!

The velociraptor reaches up with its feet and scratches at the protoceratops's face with its hooked toe claws. The protoceratops is hurt and moves away. The velociraptor jumps to its feet, snatches a baby in its mouth, and runs away as fast as it can. It will not starve today. The velociraptor wins!

The name protoceratops means "first horned face." This dinosaur was an early relative of bigger horned dinosaurs such as the triceratops, whose name means "three-horned face."

One of the most famous dinosaur fossils is of a protoceratops fighting a velociraptor. There was no winner. Both dinosaurs were buried by a sandstorm or landslide in the middle of the battle.

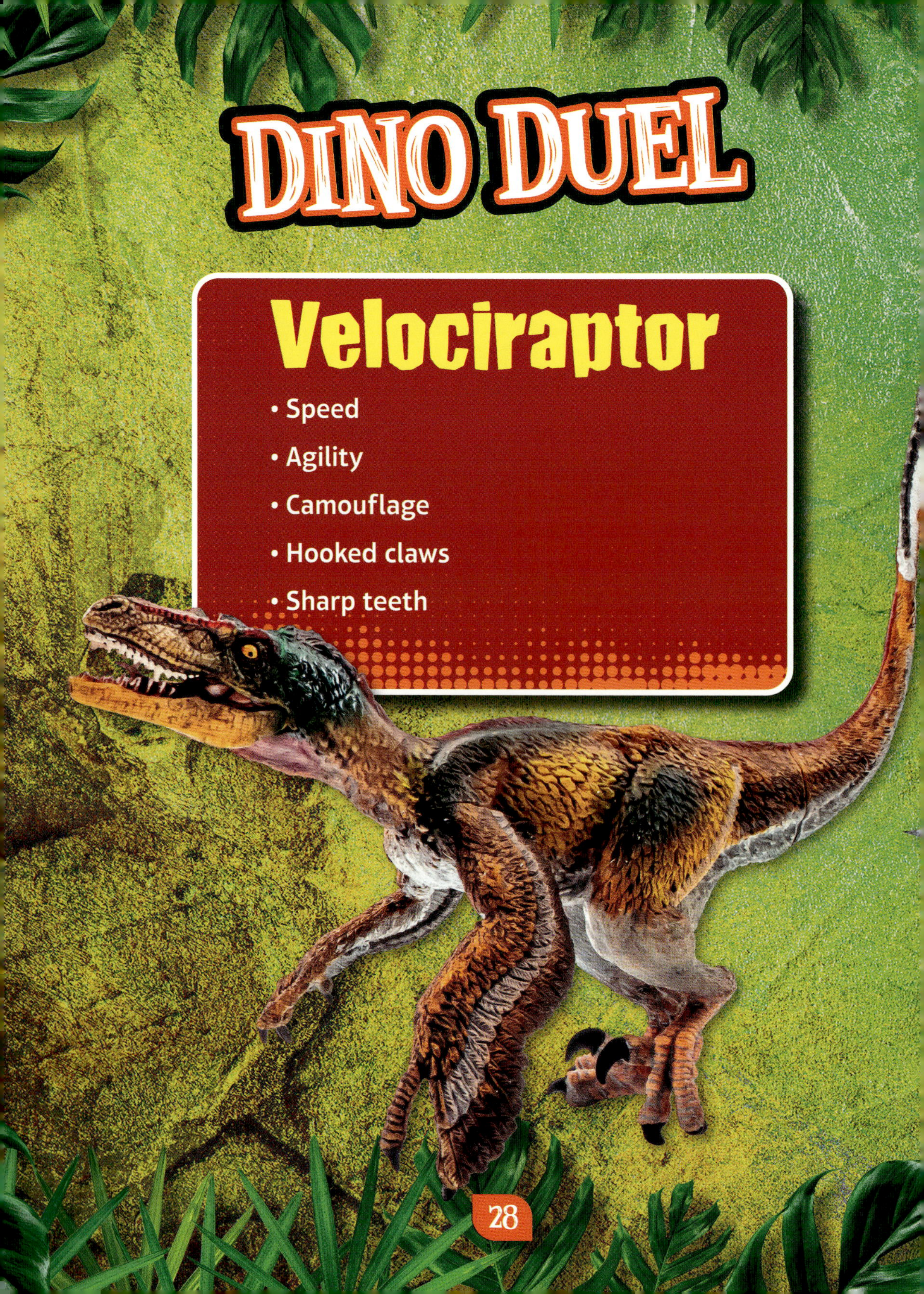

DINO DUEL

Velociraptor

- Speed
- Agility
- Camouflage
- Hooked claws
- Sharp teeth

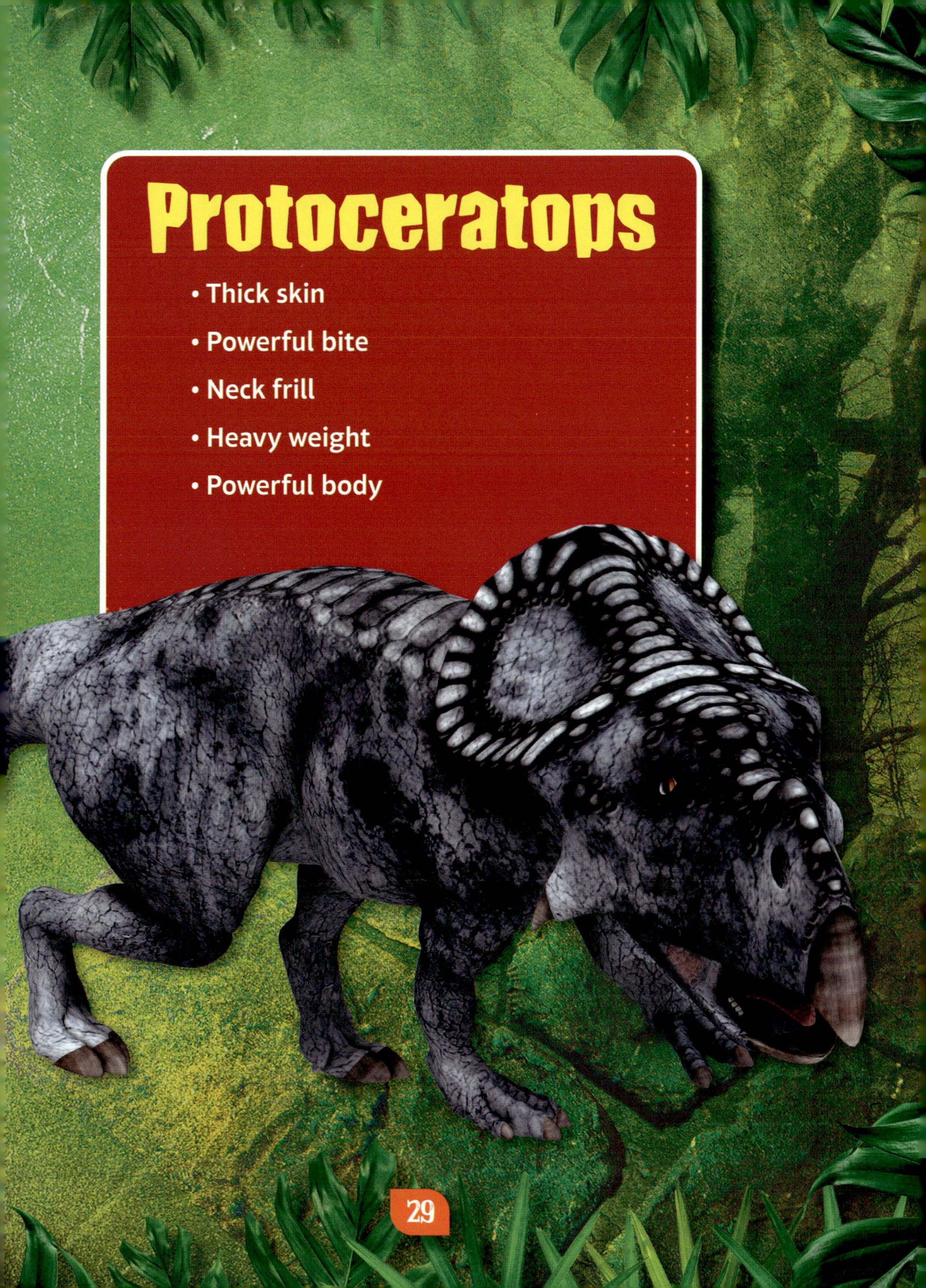

Protoceratops

- Thick skin
- Powerful bite
- Neck frill
- Heavy weight
- Powerful body

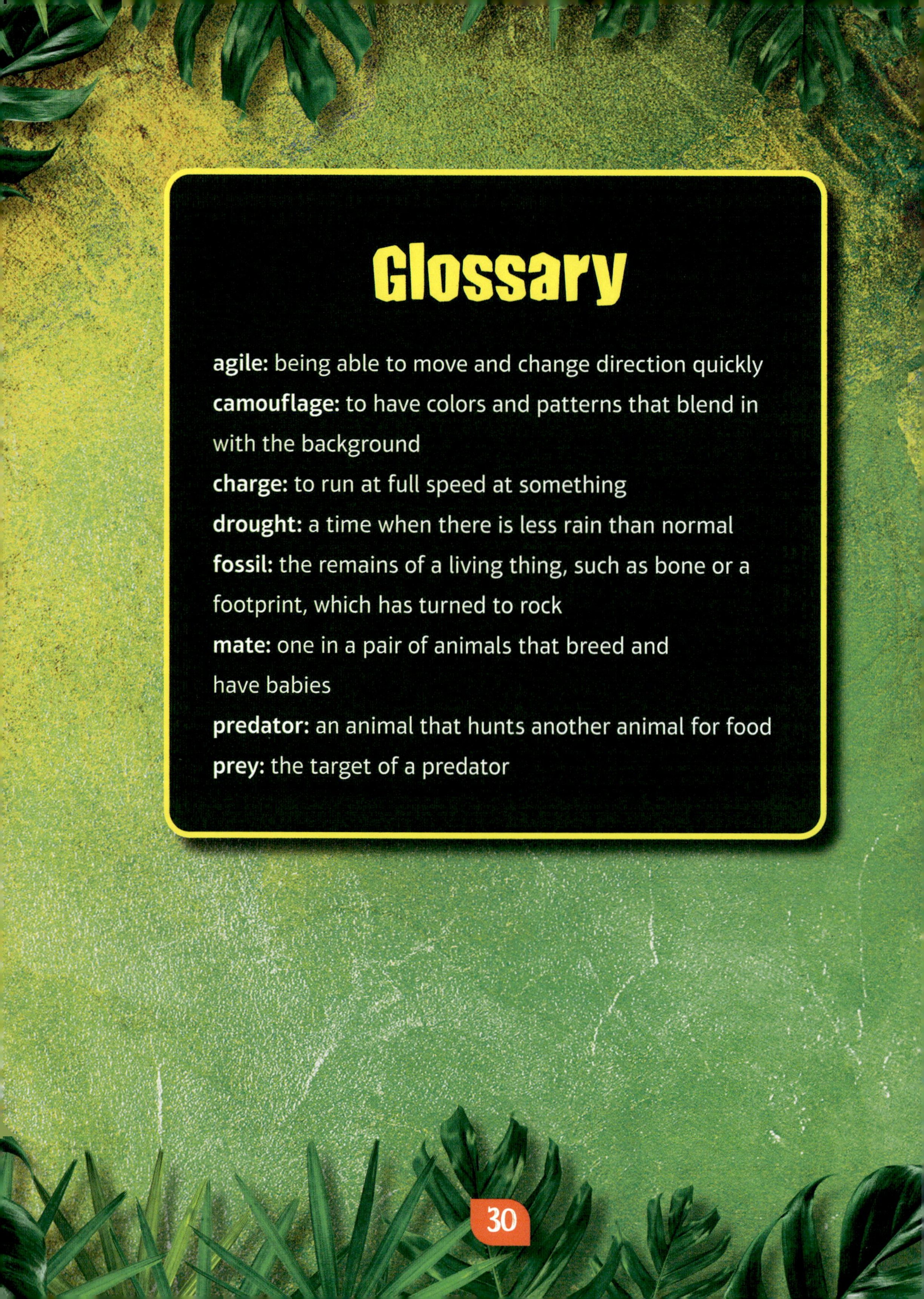

Glossary

agile: being able to move and change direction quickly

camouflage: to have colors and patterns that blend in with the background

charge: to run at full speed at something

drought: a time when there is less rain than normal

fossil: the remains of a living thing, such as bone or a footprint, which has turned to rock

mate: one in a pair of animals that breed and have babies

predator: an animal that hunts another animal for food

prey: the target of a predator

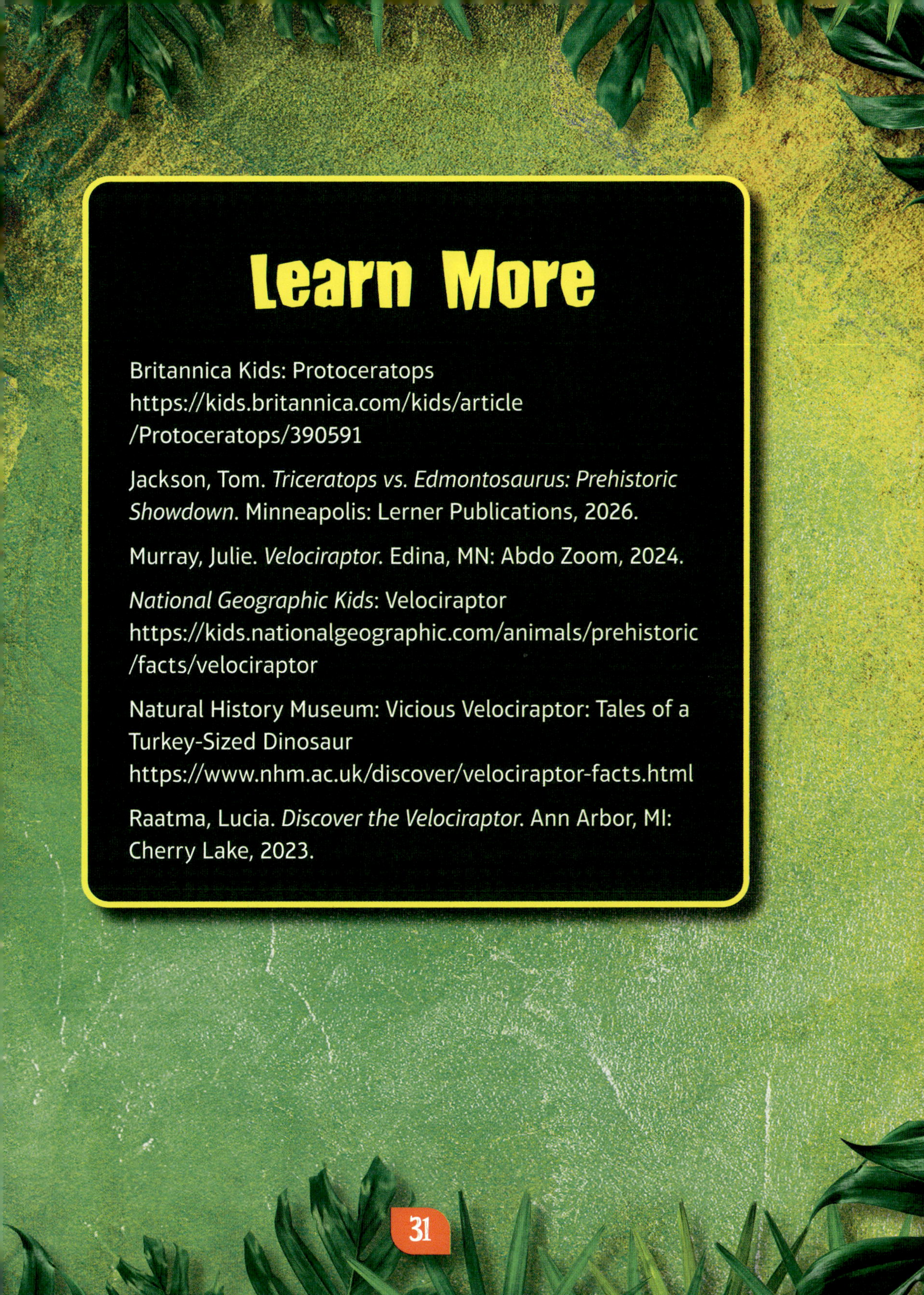

Learn More

Britannica Kids: Protoceratops
https://kids.britannica.com/kids/article/Protoceratops/390591

Jackson, Tom. *Triceratops vs. Edmontosaurus: Prehistoric Showdown*. Minneapolis: Lerner Publications, 2026.

Murray, Julie. *Velociraptor*. Edina, MN: Abdo Zoom, 2024.

National Geographic Kids: Velociraptor
https://kids.nationalgeographic.com/animals/prehistoric/facts/velociraptor

Natural History Museum: Vicious Velociraptor: Tales of a Turkey-Sized Dinosaur
https://www.nhm.ac.uk/discover/velociraptor-facts.html

Raatma, Lucia. *Discover the Velociraptor*. Ann Arbor, MI: Cherry Lake, 2023.

Index

Photo Acknowledgments

Image credits: Liidia/Shutterstock, p. 1; Lightpainter/Dreamstime.com, p. 3; N-sky/Shutterstock, p. 5; Christian Darkin/Shutterstock, p. 6; Nahuel Condino/Dreamstime.com, p. 7a; Vac/Dreamstime.com, pp. 7b, 23b; Natalia van D/Shutterstock, p. 8; Danny Ye/Shutterstock, p. 9; Ton Ponchai/Shutterstock, pp. 10, 14; Sebastian Kaulitzki/Shutterstock, pp. 11, 17; Daniel Eskridge/Shutterstock, p. 12; Dotted Yeti/Shutterstock, pp. 13, 15; Irochka/Dreamstime.com, p. 16; kamomeen/Shutterstock, pp. 18, 20; Ian Alexander/Wikimedia Commons p. 19; Mr1805/Dreamstime.com, pp. 21, 24–25; Elena Duvernay/Dreamstime.com, p. 22; Stockeeco/Dreamstime.com, p. 23a; Vac/Dreamstime.com, pp. 25, 29; Noeil/Shutterstock, p. 27; Kitti Kahotong/Dreamstime.com, p. 28. Design elements: Kompaniets Taras/Shutterstock; Chaiyapong/Shutterstock.

Cover: Liidia/Shutterstock; Kompaniets Taras/Shutterstock; Chaiyapong/Shutterstock; James Vallee/Dreamstime.com (top); Stockeeco/Dreamstime.com (bottom); Sebastian Kaulitzki/Shutterstock (bottom).